LYME REGIS
PAST & PRESENT

JO DRAPER

WITH MODERN PHOTOGRAPHS BY MIKE & WINNIE DONNO

SUTTON PUBLISHING

Sutton Publishing Limited
Phoenix Mill · Thrupp · Stroud
Gloucestershire · GL5 2BU

First published 2006

Copyright © Jo Draper, 2006

Title page photograph: A very romantic view of Lyme seafront in the 1890s shows the houses along Marine Parade peeking out from the undergrowth. The ledges off shore are visible because it is low tide.

British Library Cataloguing in Publication Data
A catalogue record for this book is available from the British Library.

ISBN 0-7509-4060-3

Typeset in 10.5/13.5 Photina.
Typesetting and origination by
Sutton Publishing Limited.
Printed and bound in England by
J.H. Haynes & Co. Ltd, Sparkford.

Dedicated to the memory of
Muriel Arber (1913–2003) & John Fowles (1926–2005)
They both loved Lyme

A 1930s view along the front, with everyone rather well wrapped up. The curtains of the Bay Hotel (left) and the lamp standard are very decorative. Beach hut roofs can be seen in the centre, as well as tents for changing to bathe. The sliver of another photograph shows how this image had been changed – Computers make it easier, but photographs were tidied up right from the 1860s.

CONTENTS

An unusual view looking along the seafront to Cobb hamlet during the Second World War – with barbed wire defences.

Looking across from Cobb hamlet with the town itself across the bay, and the rather mobile scenery beyond, 1930s. The seat on the left was popular with the fishermen – the more elaborate seat and shelter on the right was used by visitors.

One of the earliest photographs of Lyme, looking up Broad Street, and probably dating from the early to mid-1850s. Miss Turle had a girls' school near the Lion and it seems likely that she and her pupils are posed on the right. These earliest photographs have very empty streets (apart from posed people) because a long exposure was needed.

INTRODUCTION

T he camera loves Lyme Regis: Lyme is not just a seaside town, but a hilly seaside town, with outstanding scenery on all sides. And this scenery has a distinct tendency to move, with landslips a common event. Jane Austen admired Lyme's setting in *Persuasion* (1818):

with its great chasms between romantic rocks, where the scattered forest trees and orchards of luxuriant growth declare that many a generation must have passed away since the first partial falling of the cliff prepared the ground for such a state, where a scene so wonderful and so lovely is exhibited, as may more than equal any of the resembling scenes of the far-famed Isle of Wight: these places must be visited, and visited again, to make the worth of Lyme understood.

So Lyme takes a good photograph, and has been in the camera's eye since the 1850s. Some of the views taken then are still favourite spots for the photographer – like the distant curve of the Cobb (the town's harbour) or the view along the shore.

Lyme was a resort long before the camera was invented, changing from a serious port into a watering place around 1750 or a little earlier. This was lucky for the town because the harbour was too small for the large ships being used from the early eighteenth century. Being a holiday town meant that many wealthier people (with cameras) came to the town in Victorian times. Professional photographers established themselves in the early 1860s because of the holiday trade. From then on Lyme has been photographed often.

The buildings and landscape are the principal themes here: photographs graphically record the changes in what sometimes seems an unchanging town, but they also show where little has altered. Of course it is not possible to cover everything, and it seems best to try and illuminate a few areas (such as the Assembly Rooms; Mary Anning's shop; the river and the mill) rather than spread too thinly.

Lyme somehow manages to fall into a gap between Devon and Dorset (in fact it is, and always has been, in Dorset, but has made attempts at various dates to move to Devon). Lyme doesn't really care what county people think it is in, and it commands fierce loyalty from natives and incomers alike. The superbly titled *Lyme Regis – A Guide Book to Our Town* (1890) is typical. After listing all the improvements of the 1880s – the almshouses and town hall, properly restored church – the author continues:

All these blessings have been bestowed on it, with no niggardly hands, during the last few years, and have made 'Our Town', in its appearance, more worthy of the loveliness of 'Our Neighbourhood'. Among charms so many and so varied its residents reckon another, in their eyes not the least of them, – its primitive, old world condition, 'far from the madding crowd', – far enough from a railway station to be out of reach of cheap trips, which render life almost unbearable in large and more accessible seaside places: may we not truly say, that taken for all in all, little Lyme is one of the healthiest, happiest, kindliest, brightest, most loveable and most liveable of spots in all England.

This high-thinking, plain-living attitude is typical of the richer people who holidayed or settled in Lyme from the mid-nineteenth century. They enjoyed the fact that Lyme had been a fashionable resort in the eighteenth and early nineteenth centuries but they celebrated the

Looking up Broad Street soon after the Assembly Rooms were demolished in 1928, transforming the centre of Lyme. Cars were becoming more common, and the Rooms were replaced by a car park. Owens, left of centre, was the booking kiosk for his coaches.

town being too far from a railway to be really popular in their own time. Lyme tradesmen had a different attitude, and they finally managed to get a railway to the town in 1903.

From just about the same time there was an explosion in the number of photographs because postcards were invented and became an absolute mania. Being a holiday town, Lyme had even more postcards printed than inland towns. The railway brought the dreaded day tripper, and they bought thousands of cards.

With cheaper cameras from the late nineteenth century the number of photographs by non-professionals increased every year, with some views taken so often that one expects them to wear out.

Lyme Regis Museum has nearly three thousand postcards and over fourteen thousand photographs, and still there are older buildings not represented. The museum actively collects photographs and would be delighted to be given more, or offered photographs to have copied.

I have been helping to look after the photographs at Lyme Regis Museum for more than ten years, and most of them have come into the collection over that time. I thought I knew them well, but working steadily with the collection for this book has shown that I didn't really. Looking closely at all seventeen thousand images; making comparisons between photographs of different dates; carefully comparing viewpoints and thinking about photographers for this book has transformed my knowledge of them. The book has been improved enormously by the addition of new photographs by Mike and Winnie Donno.

Thanks to Lyme Regis Museum for permission to use their photographs, and to Winnie Donno, Ken Gollop and John Watts for allowing me to see their postcard collections, and use them. Thanks also to Ken, Mike and Winnie and Christopher Chaplin for reading the book and saving me from many errors, and to Sheena Pearce for word-processing.

Huge gratitude to all the kind people who have given photographs to the museum or allowed copying. Without them there would be no collection.

Lyme has been lucky in its historians. If you'd like to know more about the town there are three important books – George Roberts' *History & Antiquities of Lyme Regis* (1834); C. Wanklyn's *Lyme Regis A Retrospect* (1927) and John Fowles' *A Short History of Lyme Regis* (1982). Lyme Regis Museum stocks those which are in print, and many other booklets on Lyme, including *Lyme's First Photographers* (2006).

Jo Draper, 2006

Looking from the Cobb to the town in the 1930s (top) and the 1860s or 1870s below. Boats are the constant, but the early photograph still has a bathing machine (left). The man in sailor's uniform is probably a coastguard. The increase in buildings by the 1930s shows clearly, with the Bay Hotel (centre left) prominent.

An unusual view looking west from the road up to the Drill Hall in 1903, was taken because the owner of the camera used the house in the centre as his holiday home. Doubtless the nurse and baby, woman and dog were his too. Left, facing on to Gun Cliff, are old cottages which were demolished in the 1930s. The posh holiday house and the Curtis cottage were close together, but very different worlds.

In early photographs like this one from the 1890s, Back Beach is always full of boats, nets and other fishermen's equipment. The beach was used by the Curtis family who lived in the cottage above the beach (opposite). The pale building in the centre is the Assembly Rooms. The variety of nets, lobster pots and boats is very artistic but probably not arranged. This is really Church Cliff Beach, known locally as Back Beach.

The Curtis cottage on Church Cliff, sometimes known as Channel View, overlooking Back Beach. The Curtis's fishing stuff was always spread up the cliff to the cottage, with nets alongside the washing. The most famous Curtis was William, who lived there for the last 30 years of the nineteenth century and died aged 86 in 1907, leaving 33 grandchildren and 23 great-grandchildren. The newspaper obituary noted that 'his directions [shouted] to his faithful sons [when fishing] could often be distinctively heard for a considerable distance from the shore'. The church tower can just be glimpsed on the right. The top photograph is from 1930, taken by a holiday-maker. The middle one probably dates from the late 1940s and the bottom one is today with brand new houses to the left and the cottage extended.

The only photograph of the Baths which were built in 1805, the largest and most impressive of the three bathing establishments in the town. These were not for cleanliness, but for sea-bathing without the problems of the sea. They even offered heated sea-water. This photograph is from late in the life of the Baths – probably the 1870s. The 'soldiers' are probably local Volunteers.

The same view today: the Marine Theatre on the site of the Baths, which were largely demolished in the 1880s to make way for the Drill Hall (opposite). This was heavily adapted to become a cinema in the 1930s, and again in about 1960 when it had become the Marine Theatre.

The Drill Hall from the sea, photographed by George Vialls, the architect who designed it, soon after the 1884 opening. Built for the local Volunteers to use as a drill hall, it also had a stage and was used as a theatre right from the start. The entrance part with the tower (centre) had a reading room on the first floor.

A rare view of Gun Cliff when it was living up to its name – the square block and wall below it to the right were constructed as a gun emplacement in the Second World War as part of Lyme's defences. The photograph was taken in 1952. Marine Theatre is seen on the left. Gun Cliff had been used to house the town's guns from Elizabethan times.

The eastern part of the shore has changed a lot. Top in 1899 shows the changes about halfway through – the rebuilt Town Hall of 1889 is visible with its two towers, but in front are ancient cottages. Centre, a gap where other old cottages have already gone. On this site the Museum was to be built. The old sea walls have a gap in them.

A view after the Museum was built in 1901. Like the Drill Hall it was designed by Vialls. The sea wall has been filled in, apparently with concrete. The photograph is probably early 1920s.

A rather disorientating view straight at the Assembly Rooms from the sea. The new Museum is on the right. The photograph probably dates from the early 1920s. The big window on the end of the Assembly Rooms gave wonderful sea views, which people compared with those from a ship.

The same view in 2005, with sea defences work under way, exposing the old sea wall in the centre. All this is still changing. The museum and other buildings (right) survive, but not the Assembly Rooms.

Looking along the seafront. This is one of the earliest photographs of Lyme Regis, sometimes wildly dated as early as 1840, which seems unlikely. It was probably taken in the early 1850s, and certainly before 1862 when the feeble remains of the old fort protruding into the beach (centre) were removed. As with all the early photographs the area which was to become the Langmoor Gardens is very bare, without even trees, and looks like the landslip it is. The photographer was standing in front of the Assembly Rooms.

Marine Parade after a bad storm, with seaweed all over the beach. The fort still survives, so the photograph dates from before 1862: it is probably the aftermath of the great storm of 7 October 1857 when four vessels came ashore 'on the beach under Marine Parade . . . two of them soon became perfect wrecks, and the others though holding together are so strained as to be hardly worth repairing' (*Dorset County Chronicle*, 15 October 1857).

The seafront from a print of about 1870, probably copied from a photograph. This strange drawing somehow makes a familiar part of Lyme look unfamiliar.

The Assembly Rooms (extreme right) were tea-rooms by the time of this photograph in 1905: ladies are taking tea under an awning in front of the building, while a much more local-looking man leans on the railings outside. The seafront has been much tidied up compared to the earlier photographs and print, with railings and proper steps down to the sea. Houses have been built in some of the seafront gardens, but a large one remains.

The seafront in the 1880s and 2005. A surprising number of the houses survive – the large ones on the left, and those on the shore. The bungalow in the left centre (2005) fills what was a garden, and all the sea wall was rebuilt in the late 1970s. The machinery on the right was constructing part of the sea defences in 2005. The square white house in the 1880s photograph is Pyne House, probably where Jane Austen stayed in 1804.

A very early and characteristically empty photograph looking along Marine Parade towards the Assembly Rooms. The old fort wall which was cleared in 1862 is visible in the foreground, and a framed copy of this photograph (on glass) was packed out with newspaper dating from 1858. The photograph probably dates from around 1857–60. Madeira Cottage is the second bay window, and beyond it is a very plain row of houses with slate hanging. These were altered in the 1880s and look very different today (background right in the photograph below).

Below: The old and the new cottages, which were decorated and floodlit for George VI's coronation celebrations in 1937.

Above: Madeira Cottage, on the Promenade, gives a strong feeling of Jane Austen's Lyme, with its typical Regency bow window and pretty porch. Sir Maurice and Lady Abbot-Anderson lived there in the 1930s, and built Little Madeira cottage next door in such a convincing way that no-one realises that it is modern. This photo shows the cottage before the building works, with Sir Maurice at his porch.

This postcard from about 1922 (top) shows a very empty beach. There are a few parked cars, one with a man who is probably a chauffeur sitting and reading. The iron railings are still there in the 2005 photograph, enhanced by the new ammonite lamp standards of 2003. The Assembly Rooms complete the vista in the 1920s: in 2005 it is the round tower of the sewage/sea defence works. The house on the left (top) is Library Cottage in its original Regency state.

The seafront looking quiet in the 1860s (above) and 2005 (below). The stone jetty or groyne (Lucy's Jetty) has grown alarmingly, and the sea walls are a little different, but the scene is largely recognisable. Interesting awnings cover the seats (centre) in the 1860s view. Roland Brown noted in his 1857 guidebook 'For the convenience of those who resort to this Promenade, there are during the summer, shaded seats' from which to admire the view. Library Cottage (left) had very Regency bay windows before it was altered in the 1920s and made more 'picturesque' with a thatched roof and extensive French leadwork.

Two views looking along the shore to the Cobb, in about 1912. Bathing machines had disappeared by this time, and were replaced by neat square tents for changing. The panorama gives a fuller view of the Cobb and Cobb hamlet, but the other photograph gives a rare glimpse of a Punch and Judy show with its eager audience.

An amazing scene of shipwreck on the beach at Lyme. The ship in the foreground has *Ann Lyme* on its stern; this is probably the aftermath of the great storm of early January 1867 when four ships were blown out of the Cobb and on to the beach, including the *Ann and Emily*, a schooner of Lyme. All the ships were local, and the *Dorset County Chronicle* reported 'the shores, which are strewn with the wreck, were visited by hundreds of people'. Locals concentrated on rescuing the coal which some of the vessels had been carrying. They can be seen foraging for it all across the sands.

The reverse view (below) is of the storm of February 1974 – looking at the town and beach from the Cobb. Great contrast between the summery views with visitors and the winter storm.

Looking along the seafront back to the main town in the 1880s, and around 1950. Seven bathing machines are waiting for customers in the 1880s, painted in bright stripes. These were a leftover from the eighteenth century: a combination of changing room and supervision. In the eighteenth century bathing was medicinal, and a bathing woman would oversee the 'dipping' in sea water. By 1950 there were changing tents only in high season, and people just swam or paddled unsupervised. The sea wall here has changed a lot between the photographs.

Higher level views of the same scene, about 1870 and 2005. The rough hillside of 1870 has been walled and buildings added, but the old steps (centre) are still in the same place and are still called Bathing Machine Steps. In the print most of the bathing machines are drawn out into the water, and the 2005 photograph shows the new ammonite lamp posts of 2003.

Top: The seafront with a cart (centre) on what is always known as the Cart Road, and no railings, 1880s. *Bottom:* Soon after 1901, when Sundial Cottage was built (centre), totally changing the view from this direction. There are now railings, a variety of changing tents, and handy benches. A start has been made on the retaining walls (left) to keep the land up.

The seafront, especially what is now the Langmoor Gardens, is extremely unstable. The 1860s photograph (top) has the remains of a landslip behind the bathing machines (which have yet to be painted in stripes). *Centre:* Problems in 1926, looking into Cobb Hamlet. *Below:* Moving the slip in 1926 with the Bay Hotel beyond. This had opened in 1924, blocking the view of Sundial Cottage from this direction.

Lyme town and the harbour are separated from each other by an area which often has landslips. All these distant views of the Cobb are taken from that area, which became the Langmoor Gardens in 1913. The view takes in the whole of the Cobb. *Top:* An early view of the Cobb (1860s), with many tracks of carts across the sands. This was the usual route to the town, and indeed until the early nineteenth century the only route. Bathing machines are seen in the centre. *Bottom:* The same view in about 1892, with the Cobb still a commercial harbour, and many coastal trading ships in the Cobb.

Top: A late 1920s or early 1930s view, with formal steps up and a viewing area on top of the shelter built on the Promenade in the 1920s. The foreground is part of Langmoor Gardens. There are only small boats in the Cobb. The postcard has caught the detail of Cobb hamlet (right) beautifully. *Bottom:* A 1990s romantic take on the view across to the Cobb.

The Alice in Wonderland Garden Restaurant and Tea Gardens opened in 1946, right on the promenade with wonderful views. It was very popular, with lots of outdoor seating. Inside the building were murals based on *Alice in Wonderland*. This photograph dates from around 1960.

The Alice in Wonderland Restaurant soon after the February 1962 slip, when there was terrible destruction, with the remains of the frames for the sun awnings looking particularly odd. The restaurant always closed in the winters because so much of the seating was outside, so it was closed when the landslip happened. It was demolished soon afterwards.

On 16 February 1962 the town of Lyme had its largest and most destructive landslip of modern times. Planning permission had been granted for a row of modern flats and houses along the Promenade, and the builders had flattened an area to start building. This precipitated a huge landslip which damaged several houses, and destroyed two, including the large Cliff House. The view above is soon after the slip – see the damage down the centre. The soil in the sea was not part of the slip: it is the land moved by the builders and dumped for the sea to remove.

This photograph is a little later, after work had started to try to stabilise the slope. Huge numbers of people visited Lyme to see the landslip.

Cobb hamlet is completely separate from the town proper, because the instability of the Langmoor Gardens area meant it could never be developed. Happily the link along the front between the two has never become a proper road, although early photographs like the 1920s one above do show cars in the oddest places. The road is now barred off, as seen below in 2005. The area to the right has changed a great deal: Cobb Cliff on the right was demolished in 1959 and Wings (the chimneys peeking up beyond) in 1945. The modern building on the right in the 2005 photograph was built after the 1962 slip to help stabilise the area, and the site of Wings and the Alice in Wonderland Restaurant was made into the Jane Austen Garden.

Top: The east end of Cobb hamlet seen from the sea in 1932, with Cobb Cliff on the right, and Wings next to it. These houses had a wonderful position, and Wings was assumed for years to be the house Jane Austen stayed in when she visited Lyme in 1804. Sadly Wings had not been built in 1804. Wings has been replaced by the Alice in Wonderland tea gardens in the later 1950s view (right), but Cobb Cliff is still there.

Cobb hamlet is surprisingly dense, with houses and other buildings right on the street. It didn't start to develop until the later eighteenth century, after the Cobb was joined to the land with a causeway, stabilising the beaches. Cobb hamlet had several warehouses and pubs. The Royal Standard here has a very traditional sign, and a warehouse survives to the right in this 1920s view.

Further along the same street, but looking the other way, 1956. The stone building in the centre was a warehouse, the old Bonded Stores with vaults underneath, built in 1830. The tall building beyond is Cobb House. The Cobb Arms Garage was Lyme's earliest lifeboat house in the mid-nineteenth century.

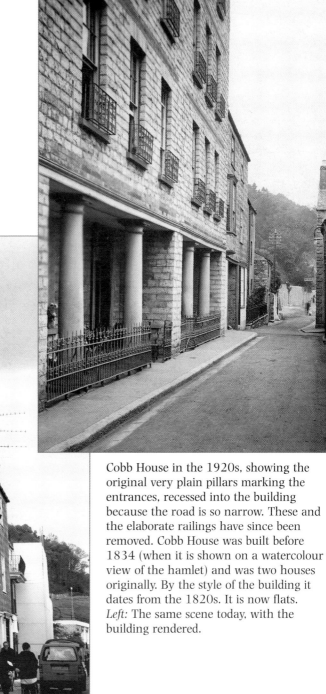

Cobb House in the 1920s, showing the original very plain pillars marking the entrances, recessed into the building because the road is so narrow. These and the elaborate railings have since been removed. Cobb House was built before 1834 (when it is shown on a watercolour view of the hamlet) and was two houses originally. By the style of the building it dates from the 1820s. It is now flats.
Left: The same scene today, with the building rendered.

Two early views looking from the Cobb into Cobb Square, with villas on the hillside beyond. Left is one of a stereoscopic pair dating from the early 1860s, when Cobb hamlet was still mostly shipping and fishing. To the left was the shipyard: the last large ship built there was the *Salacia* in 1852. By 1857 the Town Council Minutes were calling it 'the late shipyard'. By the 1880s, when the top photograph was taken, the shipbuilding yard was replaced by Ozone Terrace. The slightly different viewpoint makes Cobb House even more prominent.

This early 1930s postcard still has Marina Cottage (the small plain building right) where the Cobb Arms was soon to be built, as in the earlier views opposite. In the middle of the square is a big iron shelter which survived into the Second World War. It had originally been constructed in Edwardian times on the main promenade and was moved here after the Bay Hotel was built in 1924.

The same view in the late 1940s, with the big Cobb Arms of 1937 dominating Cobb Square, and the RAF slipway in front, built in 1937/8 and only removed in 2004.

A close-up of Cobb Square with the Coastguard posed with much equipment, around 1900. Their flagpole (white and right of centre) is prominent in early photographs. In the background is the Coastguard watch house, looking much the same today (see lower photograph of 2005) although it is now shops. It was sold by the Coastguard in 1926. On the right of the old photograph is the slate-hung Marina Cottage, demolished in 1937.

A very romantic photograph, with a large sailing vessel picturesquely drying its sails in the harbour, about 1910. By 2005 part of this view had been blocked by new buildings. The old Customs House in the town proper was lost in the 1844 fire, and replaced much closer to the Cobb by this building, which was completed in 1846. It survives today, shorn of its projecting porch and balcony (as in the 2005 view).

The foreground of this panorama from the Cobb, about 1900, looks like a stage set, with the carefully placed lobster pots. The slope behind is very bare, but by 2005 (below) trees are everywhere. Many buildings have appeared on the left in the century between the photographs.

These two views across from the Cobb show the major changes over time. The top picture dates from about 1860, the bottom one from 2005. In 1860 the Cobb was a commercial harbour, with an iron tramway (left) to help the trucks which carried lias to the ships. These were horse drawn or people pushed, so sadly there were no steam engines on the Cobb. The new Cobb Arms of 1937 blocks off much of Cobb hamlet in 2005, and Cliff House, prominent in the middle of the 1860 photograph, was destroyed by the 1962 slip. The hillside in 1860 is very bare. The 2005 photograph has the lifeboat going out on an exercise (right) with the tractor and trailer which have launched it returning to base. Yacht club dinghies are behind.

Looking out to the Cobb in an atmospheric photograph of the 1860s. The calm of 1860 is because the photographer needed everyone to keep still for the long exposure. There are several ships in the harbour, looking awkward because of the low tide.

The same view during the storm of Easter 1924, with water pouring over the Cobb from the Monmouth Beach side. Easter 1924 had started out as the hottest for thirty years, but soon changed.

A rare view across the Cobb during the Second World War. The notice reads 'THIS SLIPWAY IS CLOSED TO THE PUBLIC'. Access to the whole seafront was limited, and there were barbed wire and other obstructions everywhere. The seafront was a restricted area, and residents had to have passes to get to their homes. To the right are tank traps. The boat is the *Minister Lippens*, a Belgian lifeboat used for air-sea rescue during the war.

The same view in 2005, with the harbourmaster in the foreground. Pleasure boats in neat ranks fill the Cobb on a summer day.

The buildings on the Cobb were warehouses, but one part was used as a house. An old couple were trapped there in the Great Storm of 1824. The tramway for the lias wagons is clear along the Cobb in the 1860s view, with trading vessels moored alongside. The postcard below from the 1950s shows the Cobb when it had ceased to be a commercial harbour, but still had a few fishing and tripping boats. In both views the distance to the town proper shows clearly.

Top: The Cobb in the 1890s, with many trading ships and a wheeled crane which helped unloading. The tramway tracks have been removed. Below is the opposite view in 1942, with two Polish pilots who were rescued by the RAF. The RAF barracks are clear in the background. The boat on the right is the *Minister Lippens*.

Four views from the corner of the Cobb, the Crab Head. *Top:* early 1860s; *bottom:* about 1907. The large capstan figures in many photographs, but looks most workmanlike in the early one. The tramlines for the trucks ran through here. The bathing hut (firmly lettered BATHING HOUSE) on the Cobb appears in Edwardian times. Until the 1840s Crab Head was the end of the Cobb but the Victoria Pier then extended it eastwards.

In the background the steady westward expansion along the Promenade can be seen, with the Bay Hotel prominent in the 1930s card (above). It is unusual to see a photograph of any date with a large ship moored on the North Wall as opposite; the ship may have been moved to improve the photograph, or it may be queuing to unload because the harbour is full. *Below*: the same view in 2005.

Granny's Teeth is a favourite on the Cobb, often pointed out as the place where Louisa Musgrove fell in Jane Austen's *Persuasion*. Sadly it is disputed whether the steps existed in Austen's time. The early 1900s postcard has be-bonneted children posed to improve the picture. There was a revival of cotton bonnets around 1900, particularly for wearing at the seaside.

Right: A very unusual view of Granny's Teeth, from a postcard of the late 1940s.

An amazing coat on the southern part of the Cobb in the late 1930s with the navigation light beyond, a warning to mariners at night. *Bottom:* The Cobb from Monmouth Beach in 1946, showing a wartime pillbox in the centre: somehow a timeless photograph, despite knowing the date.

Monmouth Beach is so named because the Duke of Monmouth landed there and some of the Monmouth rebels were executed on the beach after his rebellion of 1685 failed. The big pebble beach has crept steadily further out into the sea since 1757 when the Cobb was joined to the land, trapping the shingle. This was a quiet area until about 1865 when a large factory for converting the lias into cement was built. *Top:* A view completely unrecognisable today – Albion Cottage, which was built actually on the beach in the early nineteenth century. This romantic 1860s view is confirmed by the 1841 map of Lyme which both shows and names the cottage. It is also visible in the distant view below. Albion Cottage was demolished in the 1870s or soon afterwards. *Bottom:* An early view from the Cobb, probably 1870s.

The cement factory (left) was rebuilt on an even larger scale in about 1901, just before this 1903 photograph. Ozone Terrace (right) was built on the site of the shipyard in the late 1880s. The panorama camera makes walking on the Cobb look even more dangerous than it really is.

The original caption for this 1930s photograph is 'Cob Town', and one suspects sarcasm as this view is particularly un-urban. Cobb Square is centre left (the black buildings) and beach huts line Monmouth Beach just as they do today. The buildings on the left have been demolished. The black building is the old lifeboat house after it was converted into a café. It burnt down in 1936.

A closer view of the cement factory, probably 1890s, and a similar view during the Second World War, with a defended position on the beach. The building to the right is a small remnant of the cement factory. Huts started to appear at the back of Monmouth Beach from the 1920s.

The cement factory closed in 1914 because of the First World War and never reopened. The building survived as a playground for local children until 1936, when the huge chimneys were demolished by being blown up. This was done by the Royal Engineers, and the actual detonation was announced by the Lyme Regis Town Crier. These postcards, taken from the sea, show the chimneys toppling.

The same area in 2005 – only one small building survives from the cement factory, but there are many beach huts. To the left stands the building which was the RAF barracks, now the Boat Building Academy.

Looking down Cobb Road, 1880s. This was a private toll road, built in about 1800. Until then all goods from the Cobb had to be transported across the beach. Tennis courts (left) were very fashionable in later Victorian times. The print below is also from the 1880s and must have been based on a photograph. The print maker has, as usual, widened the road greatly, and peopled it with tiny pedestrians to make the view even more impressive.

Lyme used to have several houses hung with slate. The local lias is a poor building stone and slate hanging made it more waterproof. This house in Cobb Road can be seen in the print opposite, and had scale-like slates. It was known as The Crooked House and the photograph of 1956 (top) shows why. It was on a very unstable spot, and the 1962 Cliff House slip finished it off, along with the house next door. The 1962 photograph (right) shows the demolition, with the timbers to hold the slates showing clearly.

Distant views of the Cobb are the commonest photographs of Lyme – this one from the west is often repeated because of the happy curve of the Cobb. These are the earliest photographs taken from this position, both dating from the 1860s, with carefully posed people to add interest to the foreground. The Cobb has several big ships, including one moored against the north wall, an unusual berth. The lifeboat house of 1866 is visible in the top photograph just right of centre. The other is taken from further east, along Cobb Road, and has more roofs of Cobb hamlet.

A lower level view of the 1880s gives more detail of the buildings. The lifeboat house is seen on the left and the remains of the brickyard on the right. The lower view dates from about 1900, with Ozone Terrace to the left. The brickyard has gone.

Looking down on the Cobb: top 1890s, bottom 1950s. Ozone Terrace centre is prominent in both, but by the '50s there are dozens of huts – small beach huts right on the sea, and the bowling green chalets further back (foreground). The little building right was the new lifeboat house of 1866, and survives today as public lavatories.

These long views of the 1890s (top) and 1962 (bottom) show the huge changes at the back of Monmouth Beach. In the 1890s the cement factory and the brickworks virtually fill the area: the brick kiln is the conical building in the centre. In 1962 all this has gone, and the RAF barracks of 1937 dominate, along with beach huts. The bowling green is centre left, and car parking is important.

Looking down Sidmouth Road, 1931 (top) and 2005. Coram Tower (left) was built in the 1880s as part of St Michael's College, a school for sons of the clergy. The school closed in 1899, and the huge building was renamed Coram Tower soon afterwards, after Thomas Coram of the Foundling Hospital in London. He was born in Lyme in about 1668, but soon left. In 1931 Holmbush Field to the right was still a field: now it is a huge car park. Preparations for the houses on the right seem to be starting in 1931.

Sidmouth Road becomes Pound Road as it gets into Lyme proper, and was very narrow until the 1950s.
Top: Early twentieth century, the road is narrow and, unusually for Lyme, has more trees then than now.
Most of Lyme has become more wooded since 1900. When Lyme developed as a resort villas were built
on the hillsides outside the town for the views, some in their own grounds, some (like these) along the
roads. Tivoli Cottage, the octagonal house, is often thought to be a toll house, but it is not – it is simply a
fanciful villa.

The Hotel Alexandra opened in 1901 and these two photographs of tea on the lawn date from 1907 to 1910. The Alexandra had been Poulett House, the nearest Lyme came to having a big house. It had changed hands several times in the nineteenth century, with Lyme's MP William Pinney living there, and then the Peek family. In 1902 the local guide described the hotel as 'luxuriously furnished throughout, in excellent taste . . . bathrooms and sanitation thoroughly up-to-date . . . suites of rooms are available. Both the cuisine and the wines are excellent.' The grounds, with their sea views, remain a great attraction, and one can still have tea on the lawn, as here. The back of the building faces the lawns and sea.

An advertising booklet from about 1927 gives the rates for the Alexandra – winter 4½ to 5 guineas per week all in, summer 6 to 6½ guineas. Extras seem much more expensive with an evening fire in the bedroom 2s and a hot bath 1s. Visitors' servants were accommodated at 10s 6d per day, and dogs 2s 6d, 'whether fed or not, but cannot be permitted in any of the Public Rooms'.

A contrast in vehicles outside the front of the Alexandra in 1901 or 1902 – they are both expensive: the novelty is the motor-car. This forecourt today is the car park, but cars were very rare when the photograph was taken. The Alexandra was making a statement about how up to date it was, as well as how luxurious. The car has no number plate because there was no vehicle registration until 1904.

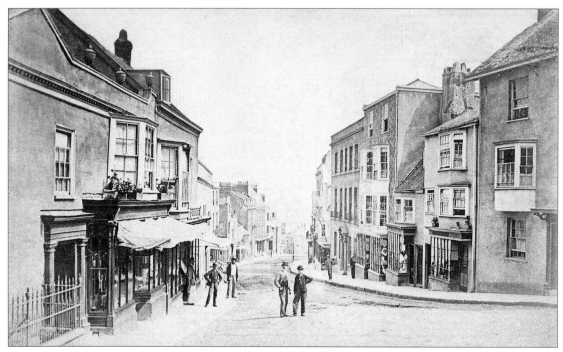

The top of Broad Street is a popular place for the view, but there can be very few small towns with so many photographs of the main street before the 1870s. These views show little change over time, with the blinds of Thornton the chemist prominent in many (left), along with the Coade stone urns on top of the building. The top picture is by William Shephard, the lower by Jonas Walter, two of Lyme's earliest photographers.

Looking down Broad Street in the later 1930s (top), and in 2005, really much the same overall as the 1860s, although a few buildings have changed. Herbert Love took over Thornton's shop in about 1895 and adapted the frontage to make it more suitable for a butcher – moving the door to one side and making the window one big pane of glass – very modern.

Top: Thornton's blinds do not star in this early photograph of the 1860s, which was probably taken in the late evening because the long exposure made people (who move) undesirable. The gas lamp right on the edge of the pavement on the bend (centre) looks like a traffic hazard. The three-storey porch (centre left) is a remnant of the Great House – a big seventeeth-century house. The porch was demolished in 1913. *Left:* A print of the 1860s, which is clearly based on a photograph, but unlike photographers print makers can twist the right-hand side of the road to make the shops more prominent.

Mary Anning, the famous fossilist, had the little shop behind the cart (with oval sign) from 1823 until her death in 1847. It was taken over by John Beer, hairdresser, in about 1870, and he and his son were at this shop into the 1930s. *Top:* 1880s; *Right:* The postcard dates from soon after 1901 when Lyme Regis finally got street numbers.

Looking up Broad Street in 1960/1 (top) and 2005 (bottom). Dunsters, with two-storey bays on the left, was still in business in 1961 – they had published most of the nineteenth-century prints of Lyme, and still had some of the 1839 landslip prints for sale when they closed. There seem to be more signs in 1960 than today, but most of the buildings survive. In 1960 parking seems unrestricted. In the 1950s the building in the centre was threatened because people wanted to replace it with a roundabout. The proposal was fought off.

The junction of Broad Street and Silver Street, 1942 and 2005. The corner building has been used for the fund-raising sign because of its prominence. Lyme has raised way over its target for 'Wings for Victory Week' – perhaps that is what the Town Crier is announcing. In 2005 the signs are much duller. The Baptist Chapel (right) dates from the early nineteenth century.

Parts of Broad Street are completely unchanged, but this area is nearly unrecognisable in the postcard of about 1900–10 (top). The little house (right) became a garage (as in the later 1920s card below) and is now Woolworths. Coming down the hill on the 1920s card is a coach – regular motor bus services to Lyme started in that decade. It seems strange to have a petrol station right in the middle of the town, but this was common into the 1960s.

The slope of Broad Street gives a problem for front doors, and this house has solved it by having steps up
to a flat platform, which forms the arch over the basement and also supports a two-storey bay window.
Top: 1860s; *bottom:* heavily decorated for 'Warship Week' during the Second World War. The ship model
is superb and probably the minesweeper HMS *Lyme Regis*.

A secret part of Lyme – one of the pedestrian ginnels off Broad Street (visible at the end), and really little changed today from this early twentieth-century view. James McNeill Whistler had his studio here when he came to Lyme for three months in 1895. He painted two famous portraits while he was here – *Little Rose of Lyme* and *Master Smith of Lyme Regis*, along with seventeen lithographs and several small paintings of the town. *Left:* 1900–10; *bottom:* 2005.

The middle of Broad Street in the early 1920s (top) and the later 1930s. One sad loss is the decorative lamp standard, replaced by a much plainer one. The Star Tea Company were general grocers as well (left, 1920s). By the 1920s there were as many shops in Broad Street as there are today – in the nineteenth century there were fewer because there were more in Church Street, Coombe Street and Silver Street.

Traffic in Broad Street. *Top:* In the 1890s, with a surprising number of carts and carriages. *Bottom:* 1911, with just one car and one horse and cart. *Opposite:* 1930s (top) with parking becoming a problem and 2005, where it certainly has become one.

The handsome two-storey bay windows of the Three Cups (left) are prominent in all the photographs. This started life as Hiscott's Boarding House in the early nineteenth century, and took the Three Cups name from the hotel in the Square which was burnt down in 1844. This causes much confusion. By 2005 the Royal Lion has taken over the New Inn next door.

Top: One of the two contenders for being the earliest photograph of Lyme Regis – the bottom of Broad Street – possibly as early as 1850. The Royal Lion has a tiny lion above the gas lamp and has no hanging sign. The photographer has avoided including people, and probably needed a long exposure. This is the Lyme Mary Anning knew. The dark stripes in the background are the ledges, which don't come that far today due to quarrying. The view below is probably the later 1850s. The man is standing by Lyme's Elizabethan water supply – an open gutter. This was steadily abolished from about 1850, with the little stream being buried in pipes. The work was done piecemeal, and it is impossible to say when each bit was covered.

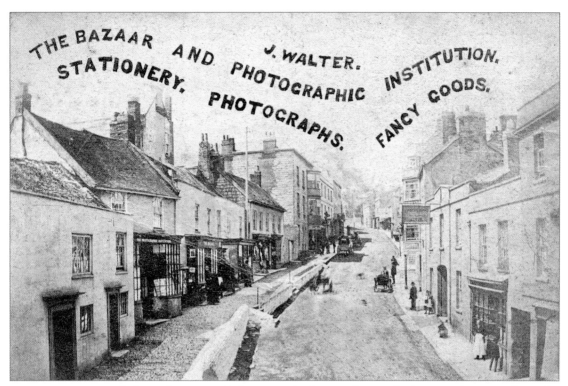

Two views up Broad Street by Jonas Walter, Lyme's first professional photographer. His shop, the Photographic Institution, was the first bay window on the left, and the one above was the Bazaar, also run by Walter. Both these views date from the 1860s. His two shops and the ones above have bay windows dating from the 1820s or 1830s when many such were added to Lyme shops.

The Royal Lion, looking very unfamiliar because of the painted olde worlde beams, presumably intended to make it look more picturesque. Really it just looks daft because the proportions are handsome Georgian, too tall and regular for a timber building. The paint job was applied in 1907 when John Grove, who had been landlord since about 1870, retired and Richard Russell took over. 'Motors' as well as livery (for horses) is advertised on the side: from 1920 the Lion was advertising a car for hire. In 1898 they were advertising only horses 'post horses, hunters, hacks and carriages of every description on hire at moderate charges'.

The Royal Lion returned to 1867 for the filming of *The French Lieutenant's Woman* in 1980. Broad Street was transformed, with the bus shelter at the bottom of the hill having to be thatched to pass muster.

The Royal Lion was a coaching inn, but after the railways started this trade declined. Until 1903 when the Lyme railway opened there was a horse bus to Axminster to join the line there. By the 1920s, when this photograph was taken, the horse bus ran only the short (but steep) journey to Lyme railway station. The notice under the porch reads 'our tea pavilion is now open on the parade'. Odd to see horse-drawn transport and a woman (left) in 'modern' dress.

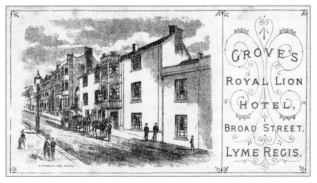

Above: An 1870s advertisement card for the Royal Lion. The reverse gives the prices – luncheon 2s to 2s 6d; bedroom 1s 6d to 4s, but with inclusive terms of 2 to 3 guineas a week. As usual with these little prints, miniature people and carriages make the buildings look huge.

Right: Filming *Persuasion* outside the Royal Lion in 1971 – one hopes the AA sign was outside the camera's view. Neither Jane Austen herself nor her fictional heroines would have stayed at the Royal Lion as it barely existed in her time.

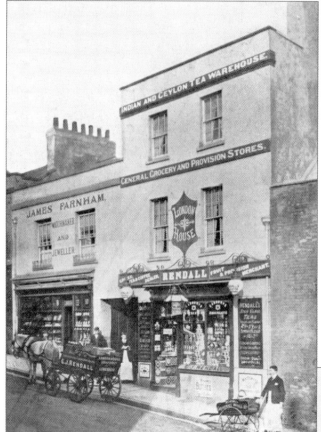

Rendall's grocery shop, Broad Street, about 1900, with the two delivery vehicles posed outside. London House painted prominently in the middle was the name of the house, not a trading link. Rendall came to Lyme in 1879 and always advertised extensively – in 1890 he was featuring 'the latest novelty; tea in MODEL LIFEBOATS'. His usual teas ('best value known, tried once, used always' ranged from 1s to 3s a pound (11 different prices). He took many photographs around 1900, including the passageway (right) behind the shop, rather a different image to the advertisement. This is now Drake's Way.

A tiny market or fair at Lyme in the 1890s, a rare image. Tuesdays and Fridays were market days at that time, and there were two fairs a year in February and September. The shops and houses behind had been rebuilt after a big fire in 1889. Wellman was a tailor.

The same view today shows many of the shops surviving, but Lyme no longer has a market. Selina Hallett remembered the fairs of the mid-nineteenth century when the area in the photograph was used for gingerbread and toy sellers, with onion carts below in the autumn.

Lyme is so mild that it rarely gets any snow,
and what comes usually quickly melts.
February 1978 was different – Lyme had
lots of snow and it stayed for three days.
There was no traffic because the roads
were blocked off, and many people
photographed the picturesque effect on
the town. The policeman seems to be
recording as well as patrolling.
The melting snow caused flooding.

The buildings in the middle of Broad Street were built on the market place. The 1844 fire destroyed the market house which ran uphill from these surviving buildings. *Top*: about 1910, with the Assembly Rooms in the gap right. *Middle*: 1930s, with a clear view of the sea because the Assembly Rooms have been demolished.
Bottom: about 1950.

The view from the Royal Lion in a late 1920s postcard, and 2005. In the 1920s the Lion's pillars are painted with marbling. The postcard was probably designed to star the building opposite as it was published by Van Allen, house and estate agents whose office is in the centre. He also owned the Riviera Private Hotel in the same building. This is Pine House, possibly where the Austen family stayed in 1804.

A classic view of Lyme through the pillars of the
Three Cups, with the buildings in the centre
framed by the sea. Jane Austen described this in
Persuasion: 'the principal street almost hurrying
into the water'. The Royal Lion is on the left.
Top: 1920s; *left*: 2005.

The Assembly Rooms (left) were in the middle of Lyme. *Top:* 1870s or early 1880s, with the Victoria Hall which was added to the Assembly Rooms in 1866. The shop in the centre has a beautiful bow window on a smooth curve, the line shown on the 1825 map of Lyme. Donkeys were used at the cement works for carrying the lias, but they were also useful for many other jobs. *Bottom:* A similar view soon after 1911 when the garage (right) was built. The shop window centre has been rebuilt with larger panes of glass and in a different shape. The coal merchant's building dates from after the 1844 fire.

Top: An unusual view looking along the side of Victoria Hall – the Assembly Rooms. Right is Bell Cliff. The band looks military, and the postcard probably dates from around 1900–10. *Bottom*: The same view in 2005, with ammonite lamp posts replacing the big lamp of 1900. There must always have been steps up to Bell Cliff. The Assembly Rooms site is a car park, temporarily fenced off for coastal protection works.

The side of the Assembly Rooms, about 1910. They were built on a prominent site in the 1770s, but by 1900 they had long ceased to be used for their original purpose, and were tearooms. From about 1915 one of the rooms became a cinema.

The only photograph of the town stocks, and an unusual view looking towards the Pilot Boat (right background). One suspects that the victim (a Curtis) is posing rather than being punished. Background left – the Assembly Rooms. The photograph is probably about 1910.

The side of the Assembly Rooms, about 1920, with waitresses peeking out and advertisements for 'delicious home made ice cream', 'hot & cold lunches' and 'Japanese Tea Rooms'. The last explains a postcard inside the tearooms decorated with fans and paper lanterns.

During the demolition of the Assembly Rooms in 1928. The building was in poor condition, and there had been problems with the sea wall in front of it, but it seems sad that such an attractive old building was lost. The railings are the ones in the photographs opposite. Lyme was hungry for car parks, and that is what the site became.

The same view in 2005 – the car park being used by the contractors for the coastal defence works. The millennium clock in the centre usually overlooks neatly parked cars, not this.

The middle of Lyme in 1844, caught just before the fire of the same year which destroyed the old Three Cups Hotel (left), the Customs House (centre) and many more houses in Coombe Street. The Assembly Rooms (roofs right) survived, as did the old shop and other buildings on the right. Before the fire this was very much the centre of the town, but the buildings were not immediately replaced, and the Customs House was moved to the Cobb. The Three Cups was never rebuilt. The old Three Cups was the poshest hotel in early nineteenth-century Lyme – in 1801 it was advertising that it had been enlarged so that 'the nobility and gentry who may be inclinable to pass a few months at Lyme will in future find that nothing will be wanting to render their accommodations as satisfactory as any watering place'. The contents were sold in 1833 and included twenty 'very good' feather beds and 'a large quantity of superior cut glass', along with lots of mahogany furniture.

A similar view in about 1900, showing (left) the plain house which replaced the Three Cups. In 1850 Lyme Town Council was complaining that the rubbish from the fire had not been removed from the site of the Three Cups, never mind a replacement built. Here low buildings for a fish market have been constructed on the site of the Customs House, and a plain house used as a coal merchants.

The Old Fossil Shop in a very early photograph dating from the later 1850s or early 1860s, when William Moore was running it. He sold fossils and curiosities as well as music and pianos. The whalebone seems to have been used as an eye-catcher outside the shop from its earliest days. *Below:* A demonstration in support of the Cement Works in July 1913, exactly when the Fossil Shop and the south side of Bridge Street were being demolished (background). Some Lyme householders were objecting to the acid dust created by the works. The 90–100 employees organised a march of support.

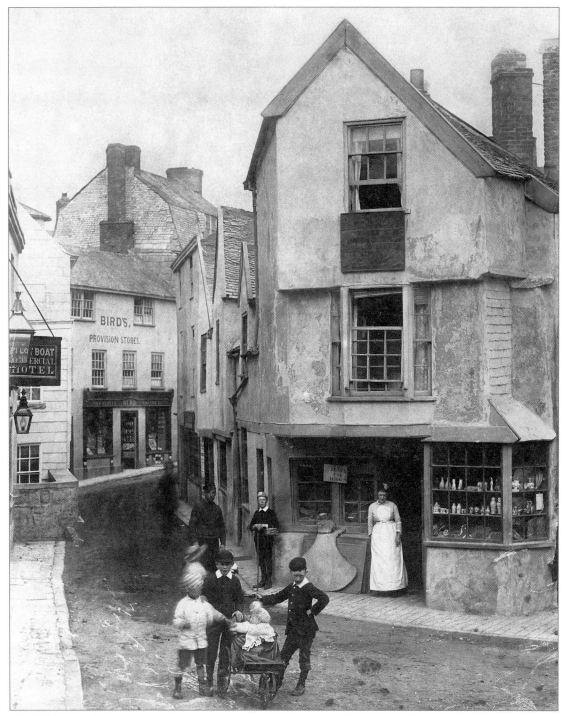

The Old Fossil Shop was a great attraction in Victorian Lyme. Above is the shop in the 1870s or 1880s when it was owned by James Dollin. Fossils and curiosities were sold side by side, with one window for each. Bridge Street was ridiculously narrow – Mary Anning was lucky not to be injured there when a cart tried to crush her in 1830. The narrowest part was only 7ft 8in wide, totally unsuitable for motor traffic, and in 1913 the whole southern side was demolished to widen the road. All the ancient houses behind the shop went, along with the equally ancient Fossil Shop.

The Fossil Shop in a closer view of about 1910 where the poor old shop looks very dilapidated. Right to the end it had 'Fossil Depot' lettered on its façade – depot was a trendy word for shop when it was established in about 1840. *Bottom:* The rebuilt Bridge Street soon after 1913, with the new shops and houses to the right.

A rare informal street scene, Bridge Street about 1900, with many children. The old houses background left were replaced in the 1930s, as seen below in the 2005 view. The shops survive – the middle one is now a fossil shop. Coombe Street is on the right. The narrowness of old Bridge Street comes over very clearly, as does the bustle of the street scene.

Laying electricity cables in Bridge Street in 1909, which must have made things even more difficult for traffic. This photograph really shows how narrow the street was. All these houses have been demolished and replaced, as the 2005 view shows. Even the widened Bridge Street is so narrow that traffic lights are needed.

Top: The original Museum had a very strange east wing, seen here at the Proclamation of Elizabeth II in February 1952. The lower part had open arches, the top an odd set of windows. It was demolished in 1968 because it was unsafe, and replaced with a much plainer top storey. *Bottom:* Bridge Street in November 1942, with a wartime parade, apparently in rain.

Top: Lyme Regis Town Hall was an unimpressive building before the 1880s, but it was then virtually rebuilt with a strange lighthousey tower and an imposing entrance. Here it is in the 1890s, before the Museum was built. The tiny house right (only 8ft wide) was demolished to make way for the museum.

Right: The same view today, with the Museum of 1901 right. The grocer's shop has become a fossil shop. The simple Georgian house in the background of the 1890s photograph has been greatly elaborated and was a hotel in the 1950s.

The corner where Church Street and Bridge Street meets is very sharp, and is at the bottom of a long hill. The poor old Town Hall takes the brunt of any accidents. *Left:* A brick lorry in the 1980s. *Below:* A 1970s coach. Many of the lorries which get into difficulties here are not even delivering to Lyme – somehow they have left the main roads and think they have to go through Lyme, which they do not.

Right: A coach in October 1999.

A favourite view in Lyme: the glimpse of the sea through the passage beside the Town Hall and through the paired windows. *Top:* before the rebuilding of the 1880s, when there was a shop on the ground floor. *Bottom:* a more distant view, with the Town Hall rebuilt. The little tower on the roof has since been removed. This postcard of about 1910 shows the Georgian fronts which survive today on the right: most of the left-hand side of the road was rebuilt in the 1920s.

A panoramic view up Church Street in 1903 with the prominent Methodist Chapel of 1839, built in a rather strange imitation Gothic – partly Norman, partly something else. This was demolished in 1978 and replaced by a block of flats.

The opposite view to the picture at the bottom of page 98, with Tudor House (then a hotel) on the left, about 1970. This situation is still common today, as buses and lorries are too wide for the narrow street.

Church Street seems to have housed most of Lyme's photographers. *Top:* William Shephard's shop in about 1905, with a goodly selection of postcards displayed outside, and many children arranged in the background. The Red Lion Inn is on the left. *Bottom:* The house Mr Griffin had built in 1924 two doors above Shephard's shop, with his display case on the street.

The middle of Church Street in the 1930s (top) and 2005. This is another very narrow street, and some of the houses (like Griffin's opposite bottom) were built set back from the road because the council wanted to widen it. Those on the left in the 2005 photograph have been set back.

The London Inn about 1870, with a decoration across the street. Second from left is a postman, and perhaps the landlord and landlady right of the door.

Two views of the Golden Hart, which are puzzles to date. The originals should date from the 1860s or early 1870s, but the sign has G. Woodman as landlord, and he wasn't at the Golden Hart until after 1875. *Right:* with a really long ladder which has moved during the exposure, and nicely placed people.

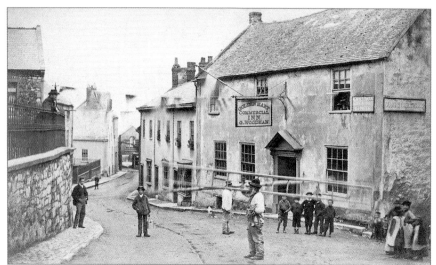

A rare view with a fisherman carrying a lobster pot. The flag must have been a traffic hazard.

The Golden Hart often described itself as 'opposite the church', and this view is taken from the church entrance, looking down on the well-dressed crowds arriving for the wedding of Constance Allen and Hugh Purvis in July 1904. This was the largest, poshest wedding Lyme had seen for a long time. The same view in 2005 shows the Golden Hart changed into the Old Monmouth Hotel. The churchyard railings of 1824 still survive on the left.

Two classic views up Monmouth Street with the church in the background. This is an old part of the town, with houses right on the pavement, and a few shops even in the nineteenth century views. *Top:* A very early view, probably 1870s. The cottages on the right were demolished in 1908. The upright picture on the left is from the 1960s – Symes was a 'high class grocer and provision dealer' (1958 Directory). The west window of the church changes completely between the photographs; it was 'restored' in 1934.

George's Square (usually called Cats Park in Lyme) in 1909, just after it was made into a tiny park. This is the reverse view from the same spot as the photographs opposite. The George, the main inn at Lyme, was on this site, facing Coombe Street, but extending backwards over most of what is now George's Square. The inn was largely destroyed in the great fires of 1803 and 1844 and its site redeveloped with houses. *Bottom:* a similar view in 1982.

Summer Hill was an elegant house built on Charmouth Road in 1819 by William Poole, a wine merchant of Lyme. He built it as a speculation, to let to visitors. In March 1819 his advertisement stated 'newly built, but the walls are dry'; four sitting rooms, six bedrooms, servants' accommodation and even a water closet. When it was advertised for sale in 1840 the views were extolled and the fact that it was 'well adapted for the Residence of a large Family of respectability', or an investment 'by reason of the Rental which it affords during the greater part of the year, from families visiting Lyme'. The photograph dates from the 1870s.

Summer Hill at the end of its life, photographed in 1987, the very year it was demolished to make way for a block of flats. The house had been rented by A.S. Neil from 1924 to 1927 as the first home for his experimental school, which moved to Suffolk but retained the original name – Summerhill.

Lyme Regis Gas and Range Company Works, off Poole's Court, about 1900 (top) and the same area today. A tiny bit of the works survives, with its original window. The first gas works at Lyme was on East Cliff from 1835, but it was moved to this more sensible inland site in the mid-nineteenth century. As the name states, cooking ranges were also made there: Edward Brown, ironmonger in Broad Street, patented an economical kitchen stove, and manufactured them in Lyme. Until 1857 they were made off Broad Street, but then the manufactory moved to this site.

Cloverdale Garage, Charmouth Road, in the 1940s: in 1935 this was Cloverdale House, bed and breakfast, in the Directory. The garage expanded and was altered, so that by 1987 it was as the photograph below. In that year it was demolished and replaced by a block of flats – Cloverdale Court.

Rose Cottage, Charmouth Road, when it was Mr Moore's Nursery. This is another photograph which has been described as taken about 1840, which is too early. Samuel Silvester Moore, nurseryman and florist, is first listed in the 1855 Directory, and the firm moved to Silver Street just before 1871. Moore died in 1862. Certainly this is an early photograph, but probably 1860s. Rose Cottage was built soon after 1841. The building in the background is at the old gas works. There are at least eight people in this photograph, but they are difficult to spot.

A view from the same spot after the demolition of Rose Cottage and the construction of Ferndown Road. The 1928 Ordnance Survey map shows this new road only half built, so the postcard must be 1930s.

An atmospheric view down Charmouth Road in 1911, with Fairfield Cottages left. They were built for the coachman and gardener to the large Fairfield House on the other side of the road. The whole group dates from the early nineteenth century, and until the 1920s they were the first buildings in Lyme coming down the hill (apart from the isolated toll house).

The same view today has an entirely different feel – in 2005 choke points were installed down the hill to slow the traffic, and the road is much wider than in 1911. The cottages survive, but are tiled now, and have fewer chimneys.

This severe bend on the old Charmouth Road was usually known in Lyme as Frost's Corner. Mrs Frost (in the doorway) sold lemonade to passers-by. The cottage was built as a toll house for the turnpike road: people had to pay their tolls here to use the road. The turnpikes had gone long before this 1900–4 photograph, but the hill must have been a real challenge for this early car. In 1927 the Charmouth Road was rebuilt on a new line above Frost's Corner, running up to the right in front of the cottage, which was demolished in the 1960s when the 1928 road was widened. The same view today is unrecognisable, with new housing.

Looking west across Lyme, top about 1914, bottom 2005. On the skyline, roughly in the middle, is Coram Towers, and the mill at Jordan is prominent (right) in the earlier photograph with the river below and other old houses. Centre is the first house to be built (in about 1913) in the area which was to become Hill Road and View Road. The modern view is from the new development known as St Michael's looking over King's Way. In 2005 View Road runs left to right in the middle of the photograph, and Hill Road up the hill on the left.

The new cemetery was laid out off the Charmouth Road in 1856, and looks very new in this photograph which probably dates from around 1870. In 2005 really only the chapels are visible – the increase in trees is remarkable, as well as the large number of houses.

Lyme finally got its railway in 1903, but the station (a terminus) was 250ft above sea-level and about a mile from the town centre. *Top:* The station in about 1910, with the Victoria Hotel (background right) which opened in 1907 and was sited here because of the station. The hotel survives, but is masked in the 2005 photograph below by trees. The line closed in 1965, and today there are industrial buildings actually on the track.

Looking from the road into the station in 1958 (top) and 2005. In the 1950s there were about nine trains to and from Axminster on weekdays. It seems unlikely that the line ever covered its construction cost. In 1898 the Royal Lion was advertising four omnibuses (horse drawn) to Axminster station daily and back to connect with the main line. The train doubled this frequency and was undoubtedly cheaper and quicker.

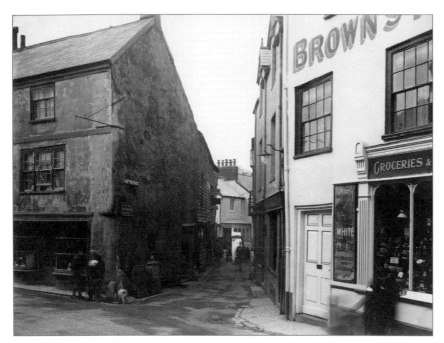

Left: Looking down Coombe Street from the Museum, about 1920. *Bottom:* The same view reversed – looking towards the Museum along Coombe Street in about 1920 (left) and 2005 (right). The weather-boarded building (right) has completely disappeared and the house on Bridge Street has been rebuilt. Lyme had many more buildings faced with timber (as here) or tiles in the earlier twentieth century.

Looking south from the middle of Coombe Street. All this part of the street burned down in the great fire of 1840, so the street is lined with plain but handsome mid-nineteenth-century houses. In fact this is probably the oldest part of Lyme, the main village street before Lyme became a town. In 1910 when the top postcard was taken there were many businesses in this area; now there are fewer.

The same view in 2005. The house on the corner (left) had been demolished in the 1930s and rebuilt with a shop on the ground floor.

View from just behind Broad Street south-east across Coombe Street towards the sea, in the 1880s (top) and 2005. In the foreground right the buildings have changed completely, but in the middle the curve of Coombe Street is clear on both. The left-hand buildings are still in the same place, and the odd tower of the Guildhall shows clearly. The right-hand tower is the Museum, not built until 1900. The other big change is the foreground: in the 1880s this was a private back yard, in 2005 a public car park.

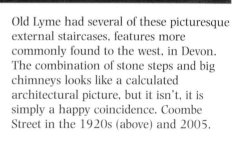

Old Lyme had several of these picturesque external staircases, features more commonly found to the west, in Devon. The combination of stone steps and big chimneys looks like a calculated architectural picture, but it isn't, it is simply a happy coincidence. Coombe Street in the 1920s (above) and 2005.

This plot on Coombe Street shows the changes in the town's needs. Originally a small house, maybe with a small shop front. In the 1920s it became the office and depot for Blue Bird Coaches, a totally new type of transport, and very significant for a seaside resort. The coaches needed much larger buildings, so by 1928 a large clear span building was constructed. This was later used as workshops and stores for other businesses, including Lyme Engineering. It is now the garage for the Bay Hotel, the hotel on the seafront. *Top*: 1920s, *bottom*: 1982.

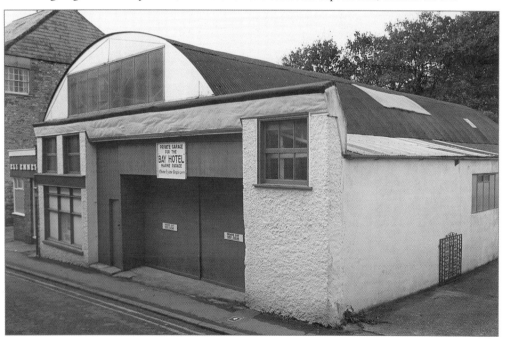

This large eighteenth-century house is directly opposite Gosling Bridge and is simply known as no. 1 Mill Green. It had been a dance school run by Miss Sarah Ann Lord in the later nineteenth century. The upper photograph shows it in the 1920s, with its original window-sashes in the middle flanked very unusually by conventionally opening ones. To the right are the ruins of a burnt house. Until the early twentieth century the lane to the right of the house was just a field entrance, but it became a proper road to new areas of housing. *Below*: the house under restoration in 2002.

Sherborne Lane shares with Granny's Teeth and the Old Fossil Shop the distinction of being the most photographed and postcarded bits of Lyme. The narrow street, especially the steepest part which had steps, is extremely photogenic. *Opposite:* probably 1880s, with urchins carefully posed. *Right:* probably about 1900 with two women posed in the doorway with a thread-winder and a lace pillow. Lace-making had been an important Lyme industry but had died out by the 1870s, so this was probably set up by the photographer. *Below:* The opposite view about 1900–10 with children for scale.

The upper and wider part of Sherborne Lane, about 1910 (top) and 2005 (below). The first reference to Lyme as a place is of 774 and is the grant of a manor and rights to take salt to Sherborne Abbey. Sherborne Lane must owe its name to being owned by the Abbey. In 1910 the road was still cobbled, and many of the cottages were still thatched. The lower part of the lane is too narrow for cars.

Further up Sherborne Lane in about 1900, with cottages on the left which have since been demolished. Foreground (left) was demolished to make way for the Baptist manse, and the others were rebuilt after the Second World War. The tall house (left, in 2005) is Eagle House.

Part of Silver Street, probably in the 1920s (top) and 2005. The shops were a fishmonger and a grocer. Broad Street is just visible in the background. These simple old houses were demolished in the 1960s. Behind them were courtyards of small houses which were demolished in the 1940s.

Silver Street from its junction with Broad Street, about 1900–10 (top) and 2005. The 1841 map of Lyme shows that the town had expanded up this part of Silver Street by then. The Baptist chapel is on the right, and really very little changed between the two photographs. This building dates from the early nineteenth century but a chapel has been on this site since 1699.

The mouth of the River Lym (known as the Buddle) from the sea is a common photograph. The river banks are turned into a canyon by the tall buildings which line each side. *Top:* A very early photograph dating from before 1867 when the buildings on the extreme right were demolished. The back of the buildings on Bridge Street form a superbly irregular skyline. *Bottom:* Soon after 1913 when the old buildings on this side of Bridge Street were demolished to widen the road, and the bridge parapet rebuilt. On the right is the Museum.

Looking downstream under the bridge to the sea in the 1890s – some of the Bridge Street houses were actually on the bridge. The building on the right (the Pilot Boat) is decoratively slate hung, to make it waterproof.

The Town Mill suffered in the flash flood of June 1890 – the swollen river took a short cut straight through the mill. Two carts were washed out to sea, and the horses were only just saved from drowning. The mill clock was washed into the yard, and when rescued had a 1½lb fish in it. This photograph was taken soon after the flood.

The Town Mill about 1900, showing many alterations over ten years. The building has been rendered, and has huge signs advertising the fact that it had been converted to a roller mill.

The Town Mill in 1982 (top) and 2005 (bottom). In 1982 the mill house (centre) was occupied. The mill had been the council depot, but by the '80s only a road sweeper was using it as a store. In 1990 the Town Mill Trust was established to save the building, and it is now completely restored and milling again, with a café, shops and exhibition gallery in the ancillary buildings.

An unusual view looking across the front of the Town Mill in the 1880s, with presumably the miller and his horse, the mill stables beyond. On top of the river cliff stands a long-gone building which looks half house (right-hand side) and half barn. Even the house side looks like a conversion, with chimney stacks inserted on the side wall. This is now a car park.

Below: Looking upriver in 1927, with the so-called Leper's Well visible (left) and Mill Green and Sherborne Lane in the background. The close-up of Leper's Well dates from about 1900–10 (right). Lyme certainly had a hospital for lepers because there is a note about its repair in 1336 which shows that it had a bell tower. Early historians of Lyme seem to have decided that because the Great House in Broad Street had a tower, it was the remains of the Lepers' Hospital, and therefore the well (or rather spring) in the Great House garden was thought to be the Leper's Well. In fact right up to the mid-nineteenth century this area was called Fountain Garden. Lepers' hospitals were for those with skin complaints, sensibly thought to be contagious in medieval times, so the hospitals were placed outside the towns. So sadly this is not the Leper's Well.

Looking downstream, with old houses surviving on the left, probably 1880s. The Leper's Well is background centre, in the greenery. The river proper is down in its deep bed to the right; the higher stream here is the Lynch, the artificial channel leading to the mill. Putting small children into white pinafores must have led to a lot of washing.

Looking upstream, with the little bridge to the houses. *Top:* 1880s, with the Angel Inn (centre background) still thatched. *Bottom:* About 1910, and the Angel is totally rebuilt.

Looking down the Lynch, 1912. The old houses (left) have disintegrated but the little bridge over to them survives. This view shows clearly the river (right) and the higher level of the Lynch.

The view from Gosling Bridge towards Coombe Street with Harris & Quick's lorry beside the old building on the Lynch, about 1957. They restored it soon afterwards.

An unusual view at the bottom of Mill Green, with Coombe Street and Gosling Bridge just to the right. Clearly a convivial meeting place in the photograph of about 1910 (top); it is much quieter in 2005 (bottom). The telegraph pole is in the same place but the house (background) has been replaced by garages.

Two views of Gosling Bridge just after the Great Flood of June 1890 (top and top, opposite). The river was 15ft deep here at the height of the flood which completely removed the parapets. The higher stream (right, this page) is the Lynch, mill leat, the actual river left. The thatched Angel Inn is visible top left; the little building (right) is having its tiles removed. *Bottom*: another flood, looking downstream from Gosling Bridge in July 1926. The Lynch is pouring over into the river.

Looking downstream to Gosling Bridge after the 1890 flood (top) and the same view in 2005 (bottom). Most of the houses survive, and the rebuilt corner house on the left is clear in 2005.

Further upstream, looking along Jordan, this cottage seems to have been built actually out into the river, and was demolished in the late 1920s – its footings can be seen in the 2005 photograph opposite. This stretch of river below the cottage was also the roadway, a long ford from above the cottage for 120yds down to yet another mill, now Jordan Flats. This is thought to have been the longest ford in England.

Looking downstream at the cottage as opposite about 1910–20 with the mill (left) and other buildings in Mill Green (background), and the ramp down to the ford especially clear in the 2005 photograph foreground left (bottom). There seem to be even more trees in 2005.

Looking up the river from Jericho. *Top*, probably 1880s; *bottom*, probably 1900. In the background is Higher Mill, now flats, and two old cottages (right) which have become more dilapidated between the photographs. The railings have been much improved, however. The further cottage had a big external staircase.

The same view as the photographs
opposite, with the little waterfall and
Higher Mill the constants. Windsor
Terrace was built here in the 1920s.
The left-hand side of the river was known
as Paradise Fields – like Jordan this name
comes from the early Baptists.
The picture above dates from the 1930s,
the one on the left, 2005.

Two favourite views for the end of the book, symbolising both entering and leaving Lyme at Ware Cliffs. *Top:* The man stands on the county boundary called Devonshire Hedge: a beautiful postcard of around 1900. *Bottom:* A little later, the same area, looking back towards Lyme which is concealed behind the little rise in the background. These fields have gone on falling into the sea and parts have become overgrown since the photographs were taken, but otherwise little has changed.

'a very strange stranger it must be, who does not see charms in the immediate environs of Lyme, to make him wish to know it better'

Jane Austen in *Persuasion* (1818)